Judith Blacklock's Flower recipes for
SPRING

The Flower Press

Published by
The Flower Press Ltd
3 East Avenue
Bournemouth
BH3 7BW

Text Copyright © Judith Blacklock, 2007

This first edition published 2007

The moral right of the author has been asserted.

A CIP catalogue record for this book is available from the British Library.

ISBN 13: 978 0 9552391 2 0

Design: Amanda Hawkes

Printed and bound in China by C & C Offset Printing Co., Ltd.

Contents

Introduction

Spring is the season of inexpensive but glorious flowers that bring colour and life into the home. Spring flowers such as daffodils, tulips, *Ranunculus*, and *Muscari* love water, need little care and are ideal for simply placing in a vase.

There is a whole spectrum of spring flowers available, many of which may grow in your own garden. I encourage you to be bold with colour and texture and inventive with your containers and mechanics – there are no limits to what you can do with a bunch of beautiful blooms, some fresh water, and a little imagination.

This book, the second in the series, contains 48 designs using simple ingredients, a few techniques and a bit of style. If you are a beginner you do not need to be creative to follow the step by step instructions. If you do not have the specific flowers or containers mentioned, I hope my notes will enable you to adapt what you do have to re-create a similar arrangement. If you have more experience the ideas may inspire you to adapt the designs and make them your own. As a teacher of floral design for many years it is the greatest compliment that my ideas are taken, developed and enjoyed.

Judith

Lime keys

Lime keys are susceptible to strong March winds and on a spring walk can be collected to create an easy design for the home.

Method

1 Choose a bowl that will harmonize with the lime of the keys. The richness of this blue is ideal but you could also choose terracotta, black, deep red or orange.

2 Fill your bowl about one third with water and mass the keys in the bowl.

3 Cut the flowers short and thread through the keys into the water.

You will need

· low bowl
· lime keys (*Tilia* winged seedpods)
· a few flowers such as early *Centaurea*
· bunch of flexible stems such as dogwood, willow, birch or *Clematis*

Design tip

Lime green is a colour that will go with anything. Here the sharp contrast of colour emphasises the freshness of the lime keys.

Simply rhubarb

Rhubarb is both delicious and decorative. This unusual, seasonal container is quick and easy to make and will last for a week if kept cool.

Method

1 Place the rubber band half way up the vase.

2 Tuck the rhubarb stems under the rubber band so that they abut closely.

3 Take the lily grass and wrap over the rubber band. Place a small blob of florists' fix or Blu-tac® under the leaf at the back to keep it in place on the rubber band.

4 Fill the container with water and add your flowers in a profusion of colour and movement.

Roses and lilies

A sophisticated but simple design that only takes minutes to create.

You will need

- glass bowl that is wider at the top than the base
- pinholder
- *Aspidistra* or *Phormium* leaf
- florists' fix
- stem of a good quality lily. The lily used is an oriental lily, *Lilium* 'Pompei'.
- 7 roses. The rose used is *Rosa* 'Avalanche' which has a large head.

Design tip

The pinholder used is 7.5 cm (3 in) in diameter. These are not as commonly available as the 5 cm (2.5 in) which will also work well – you just need to keep the stems closer together.

Method

1 Attach a small amount of fix at intervals to the side of the pinholder. Cut the leaf so that it is the right size to wrap around and hide the pinholder. The fix will keep it in place.

2 Position the pinholder in the centre of the bowl.

3 Cut the opening flowers off the main lily stem but keep the secondary stems long. Place the lilies in the centre of the pinholder.

4 Cut the roses so that they are lower than the lilies and place in a circle around the lilies.

5 Add water to cover the pinholder.

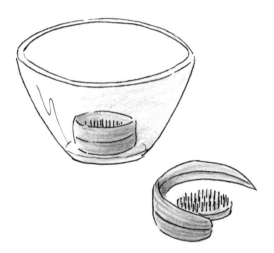

You will need

- **vase with a wider opening than the base**
- **5 cm (2 in) gauge chicken wire. For a suitable amount see Techniques page 96.**
- **5-10 stems lilac (Syringa)**
- **late spring flowers. I have used peonies, roses and Phlox.**

Design tips

Lilac is unhappy in foam but if you remove all the leaves before placing in water it should last well.

Lilac from the florist is usually sold with a sachet of special cut flower food. Do use this as it wll help to prolong life.

It is best to cut or purchase lilac when a few of the tiny flowers on each stem have opened. If the stems have been cut too early they will probably not develop.

Spring profusion

The blooms of late spring are combined here to create a mass of colour form and texture.

Method

1 Take the chicken wire and crumple to fit the container.

2 Place the wire in the container so that the cut ends are uppermost. These can be wound around strong stems to give additional support.

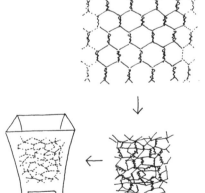

3 Take all the leaves off the lilac stems and position in the vase. The height of the stems above the rim should be about the same as the height of the container. Create a general shape with these stems and then add the remaining flowers within the structure of lilac.

You will need

- 2 low glass containers, one smaller than the other. Both of those used in the photograph have convex sides. You could however use containers with straight sides.
- birch branches just starting to leaf
- 1 stem spray roses
- 1 stem cherry blossom
- 1 stem *Ranunculus*

Design tip

The young delicate leaves of the birch are ideal for this design. If you have a garden then do consider growing a birch. They are beautiful, gracious trees and have particularly interesting bark.

Twisted birch

The flexible branches of young birch are ideal for this style of design.

Method

1 Take the flexible stems of birch and cherry blossom. Wrap them around each other to form a circle and insert around the rim of the larger container. Add water.

2 Take one further stem of birch and wrap this around in your hands to fit inside the smaller container. Add water.

3 Remove the flowers with their secondary stems from the main stem of the spray rose. Add to the swirl of plant material in the outer container so that the roses repeat the circular movement.

4 Cut the *Ranunculus* short and allow them to float happily in the smaller container.

Swirl of broom

Broom (*Genista*) is an early spring flower at the florist which blossoms later in the garden. Here a swirl of stems is simply combined with a thick church candle.

You will need

- 2 circular glass containers. My inner container is circular but tapers to the base but this is not a requirement. The two vases only need to repeat the overall shape.
- 2-3 stems broom (*Genista*)
- thick church candle

Design tip

When the water has been absorbed by the broom do not add any more. The broom will dry slowly in situ and retain its appeal for many months.

Method

1 Place the smaller container inside the larger.

2 Pour a small amount of water into the outer container.

3 Wrap the broom into a swirl that will fit into the outside container.

4 Place the candle in the inside container.

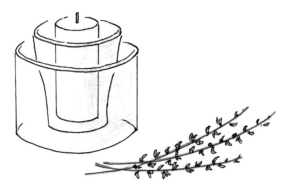

Hypericum heart

You will need

- **2 long lengths of medium/ heavy gauge wire**
- **4-5 stems of red *Hypericum***
- **stem tape**
- **red rose**

Design tip

You could either combine the hearts with a single rose as a gift or add to the base of a pot plant to give extra interest.

For a bigger heart use a heavier gauge wire.

A simple Valentine's token that you can make as large or as small as you wish.

Method

1 Bend a length of wire in half – this will be the centre of the top of the heart.

2 Thread the berries onto one end of the wire, pushing them up to the bend you have made. Make sure that you thread the berries onto the wire, narrow end first.

3 When you have reached your desired size, thread berries onto the other end of the wire, narrow end first. Curve to make a heart shape.

4 When your heart is equal on both sides, thread one berry onto both ends to complete the heart. Tape the two exposed ends of the wire together. Add extra wire to extend the stem if necessary.

4 Position the red rose centrally and tape to the stem to secure.

Complementary colours

You will need

- **low flat bowl or dish**
- **small piece of foam**
- **5-7 bunches of grape hyacinth (*Muscari*)**
- **5-7 orange double tulips such as 'Princess Irene'**
- **ming fern (*Asparagus umbellatus*) or other small leaved foliage**

Design tip

Like many spring flowers *Muscari* will grow towards the light. You may find that their heads all 'stand up' but this adds to the charm of the design.

The contrast between the opposite colours of blue and orange makes this design a striking centrepiece.

Method

1 Place the soaked foam in the centre of the dish. Add a little water in the bottom of the bowl.

2 Arrange the *Muscari*, together with their leaves, around the edge of the dish with their heads resting on the rim. The stem ends do not need to be in foam, only resting against it.

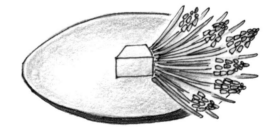

3 Partially cover the foam with ming fern.

4 Position the tulips through the ming fern.

Bowl of blue

An unusual way of displaying hyacinths that shows off their beautiful blue stems. If you can, match your flowers to your container for a stunning burst of colour.

You will need

- **low glass dish**
- **10-15 hyacinths**

Design tips

If you want your stems to be flexible, leave them out of water for several hours before arranging so they become flaccid.

Hyacinths are now available in a wide range of colours. Try pink in a slate grey dish or apricot in a low blue bowl for a strong colour contrast.

Method

1 Remove the leaves from the hyacinths carefully so that you do not tear the stem.

2 Place the hyacinths around the edge of the bowl, layering the stems over each other. This will naturally create a spiral of stems.

3 Add some water to the bottom of the dish, making sure that each flower has its stem end submerged. Keep the dish topped up with water.

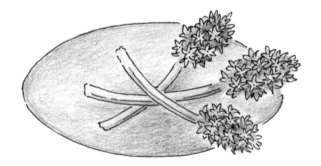

Celery submerged

Celery loves being in water so it is the perfect vegetable for this design. Its texture contrasts beautifully with the muted roughness of the lichen twigs and both are complemented by the colours of the anemones.

You will need

- **tall straight-sided glass container**
- **smaller straight-sided container that fits inside the larger with approximately 2.5 cm (1 in) gap between them**
- **piece of soaked foam (may not be necessary)**
- **12-15 lichen twigs**
- **12-15 sticks of celery**
- **about 20 anemones**

Design tips

If you have long stemmed flowers use a jam jar or other container in place of the foam.

Rhubarb is also happy under water. See the design on pages 4-5.

Method

1 Cut a circular piece of soaked foam to fit the inside of the tall container so that there is space all around for the insertion of the twigs and celery stalks. The foam will give the anemones additional height.

2 Insert the celery and lichen twigs in the gap between the two vases, alternating them all the way round. Make sure you use the celery with the concave side facing inwards so that it sits comfortably. Use the straightest twigs you have available. Give the lichen twigs a shake before you add them so that they do not dirty the water.

3 Add water and arrange your flowers to give pleasing proportions.

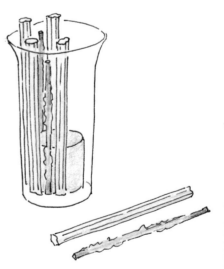

21

You will need

- **thin straight sided container**
- **thin shoots of dark red dogwood (*Cornus*)**
- **two rubber bands**
- **5-7 calla lilies (*Zantedeschia*)**

Design tips

Cornus is an easy shrub to grow in the garden. If pruned hard in the spring it will produce new growth that has brilliant colour.

As an alternative, use double daffodils in the container or a lichen twig surround with forget-me-nots. See page 42.

This organic container is easy to create and will last for months – simply replace the flowers regularly.

Method

1 Stretch the rubber bands over the container so they are well spaced out.

2 Place the *Cornus* underneath the rubber bands until you have covered the container. Push the stems tightly together from time to time to ensure you get no gaps. The finer tips should rise above the rim of the container.

3 Pour water into the container and add your callas at varying heights.

Aspidstra curl

One leaf and two flowers make a stunning, simple design.

Method

1 Take the stem of the *Aspidistra* leaf and bring it over the front of the leaf and then down through the centre.

2 Fill the container with water and place the stem of the leaf in water in the container.

3 Cut the mini *Gerbera* short and slip though the slit in the *Aspidistra* leaf created by the stalk.

You will need

· **small container with a narrow opening**
· ***Aspidistra* leaf**
· **2 mini *Gerbera***

Design tip

You could use roses, marigolds or any other round flower that will not overwhelm your small container.

Tulips in a bowl

You will need

- **large fishbowl vase**
- **thick gold aluminium wire**
- **5 parrot tulips**

Design tip

The tulips will last well in their own mini eco-system. Even when the flowers dry and curl they still have their own beauty.

This design utilises the natural curve of the tulips. The aluminium wire provides an unusual and decorative way to keep stems in place.

Method

1 Twist the wire into a mass – you may wish to curl the wire around a thick pen to create spirals, or prefer a more natural looking tangle. Place this in the bottom of the fishbowl.

2 Cut the tulips to graduated lengths and insert them through the wire, around the edge of the bowl.

Rhythmic amaryllis

You will need

- 3 identical vases, heavy enough to support the stems
- 6 stems of amaryllis (*Hippeastrum*)
- flexigrass

Design tips

If you cannot find flexigrass then use bear grass (*Xerophyllum tenax*) or steel grass, cutting off the softer, more flexible tip if necessary.

Only fill the containers about one third full with water and add more when necessary as amaryllis last longer in shallow water.

An easy way to turn a simple vase arrangement into a large scale design statement.

Method

1 Fill the vases one-third full with water. This will help to give ballast.

2 Arrange the amaryllis in the three vases so that they are balanced and even.

3 Insert one end of a stem of flexigrass into a stem of amaryllis, then curve and insert it into another. Insert further stems in a similar manner until you have created a rhythmic link between each stem.

Egg-stravaganza

It is a tough job resisting the chocolate eggs in this design but the results are well worth it!

You will need

- small cube vase and a smaller vase or tumbler to fit inside
- several bags of mini Easter eggs
- 15-20 pink *Ranunculus*

Design tip

There are many different types of chocolate egg available at Easter. Here I have used sugar-coated eggs but this design would also work with those wrapped in foil.

Method

1 Place the smaller vase inside the larger and secure with fix if necessary. Add water.

2 Fill the gap between the vases with mini chocolate eggs. Make sure they do not get wet as this will affect their colour.

3 Arrange the *Ranunculus* in water in the inner vase.

Viburnum opulence

You will need

- tall, dark coloured container
- 6-10 stems of two-headed *Viburnum opulus* 'Roseum'
- 12-15 dark purple anemones

Design tip

Avoid cutting *Viburnum opulus* 'Roseum' on the green secondary stem. Instead cut on the woodier brown stem. The green part of the stem is the current year's growth and will not last when cut. The brown part is last year's growth and is far more resilient. This tip also applies to lilac (*Syringa*).

The stunning combination of pale green *Viburnum opulus* 'Roseum' and deep purple anemones is beautifully complemented by a smooth, dark, contemporary container.

Method

1 Create a structure using the *Viburnum*. Make sure their volume is one and a half times that of the container (Techniques page 93, Proportion).

2 Add your anemones evenly throughout the design.

Bearded *Iris*

You will need

- **rectangular container**
- **floral foam**
- **10-20 bearded iris (*Iris pallida*) – the number will depend on the size of the container**
- **smooth textured, flexible leaves. I have used red *Cordyline* leaves.**

Design tip

The smooth leaves contrast well with the intricate form of the flowers but you could alternatively use flat stones, gravel, slate or flat or bun moss at the base.

This design uses bearded iris (*Iris pallida*) with its strong bold form and rich colours and texture. It is not commonly seen at the flower markets but it is an easy flower to grow in the garden. If purchasing from the florist, the ubiquitous *Iris reticulata* would also work well.

Method

1 Ensure the container is watertight. Place soaked foam in the container so that it does not rise as high as the rim.

2 Cut the stem ends of the *Iris* and place in rows. The height of the flowers should be about one and a half times the width of the container.

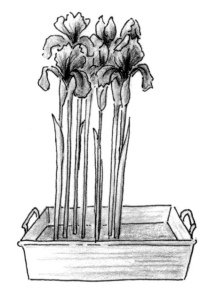

3 Cut off the stem and the inflexible part of the smooth leaves. Cut the remaining leaf into sections, sufficiently long so that they can be rolled without support. If you are worried they may become unfurled place a small amount of fix on the underside of the leaf to secure. Place these rolls of leaf on the foam to cover.

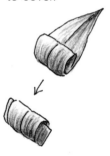

You will need

· round stoneware container
· 8-10 white frilly tulips
· 8-10 pale pink parrot tulips
· 3-4 sprays of white or pink broom (*Genista*)

Design tip

A round vase that has a relatively small opening at the top can be difficult to use as you may not be able to add as many stems as you would wish. Flexible sprays of flowers (such as broom), or foliage (such as *Eucalyptus*) have natural movement and by flowing down will soften the line of the rim and help create good balance and proportion.

The assorted tulips and broom (*Genista*) in this design pick up the subtle hues of the stoneware container and provide an exciting array of textures.

Method

1 Fill the container one third with water.

2 Take each stem of broom and cut into shorter sections – 2 or 3 from each stem.

3 Remove all flowers that would be beneath the water level. This is most important as it reduces the deterioration of plant material which takes place rapidly under water.

4 Create a volume of plant material that is approximately one and a half times that of the volume of the container (Techniques page 93, Proportion).

5 Cut the tulips and thread through the broom so that they are contained within the volume of plant material created by the broom.

6 Ensure there is always a supply of water in the vase.

Sea shells

You will need

- **round glass container**
- **15-20 *Ranunculus***
- **7-10 tulips. This design uses the fringed tulip but single or double tulips would also work well.**
- **large shells**

The touch of pink in the shells is picked up in the blowsy form of the *Ranunculus* and the delicate fringed tulips.

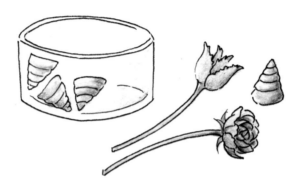

Design tip

Any kind of shell or aggregate can be placed between the two containers but the sophistication of the design suggests the use of only one type of shell rather than a mixture.

If you are short of shells, place a jam jar in the centre of your container and only fill the space between the two with shells. Place your flowers in the jam jar.

Method

1 Fill the container with shells.

2 Add water.

3 Cut the stems of the flowers and thread through the shells. The shells add support and act as your mechanics.

Mother of pearl

You will need

· **low square or rectangular dish**
· **piece of soaked foam**
· **mother-of-pearl shells**
· **1 stem of** *Astrantia*

Design tips

Astrantia **dry well. Simply leave the stems in wet foam and many will turn into everlasting flowers.**

Alternatively use the individual heads from one stem of *Dendrobium* **(Singapore orchid).**

The individual heads from a single stem are combined beautifully with the mother-of-pearl shells in a novel and contemporary style.

Method

1 Place a small amount of foam at the bottom of the dish.

2 Insert shells vertically in the foam to fill the dish.

3 Cut the individual flowers from the *Astrantia* stem. Ensure that the flowers have the longest secondary stem possible. Insert the stems in the foam so that the flowers peep over the shells.

Bluebell wood

You will need

- long slim trays
- floral foam
- twigs and stems. These should be reasonably straight. I have used lichen covered dry stems as the principal twigs.
- round leaves and short mixed foliage for the base
- spray foliage. I have used *Bupleurum* but you could use myrtle (*Myrtus*), box (*Buxus*) or a neat *Hebe*.
- ladder fern
- bluebells (*Hyacinthoides hispanica*)

Design tips

This slim design could be repeated to create a continuous line along the centre of a table.

For the containers you could use a product by OASIS® called a Table Deco (see Glossary).

The native British bluebell (*Hyacinthoides non-scripta*) is one of the most glorious sights in the woods in spring. Here I have tried to create some of the atmosphere using cultivated Spanish bluebells (*Hyacinthoides hispanica*). Do not pick wild bluebells for however good an arranger you are they look more beautiful growing naturally.

Method

1 Place the soaked foam in the trays.
2 Position the twigs and stems two thirds of the way back in an irregular straight line along the length of the foam. If you are planning for this design to be viewed from both sides, position them along the centre line.
3 Cover the foam and sides of the container with round leaves and mixed foliage cut short.
4 Add the ladder fern and spray foliage.
5 Complete by adding bluebells.

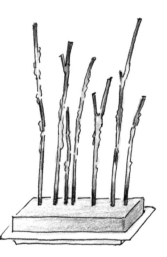

Forget-me-not

You will need

· straight sided container
· lichen covered branches
· 2 rubber bands
· raffia
· forget-me-nots (*Myosotis*)

Design tip

Forget-me-nots that grow in the garden have short stems but its close relative *Borage* has much longer stems and is just as effective if its rather dominant leaves are removed. The leaves will make excellent compost.

The woodland harmony of forget-me-nots and lichen covered twigs create a design to lift the spirits.

Method

1 Place the two rubber bands over the container so that they are at a distance from each other.

2 Tuck the twigs between the container and the rubber bands.

3 Tie raffia over the rubber bands.

4 In the hand mix the remaining twigs and the stems of forget-me-nots to make a pleasing mixture.

5 Place the twigs and flowers in the container filled with water.

Spring assortment

A pretty mass of seasonal flowers that shows the abundance of colours and textures available during the spring.

Method

1 Create a grid over the top of the container using adhesive tape (Techniques page 95). Hyacinths have thick stems so make sure the holes are not too small.

2 Add your flowers until you have an even balance of colours and textures.

Early flowering *Magnolia*

You will need

· low round glass bowl
· 2-3 stems birch (*Betula*)
· 3 *Magnolia* flowers
· small coloured glass container
· 2 tulips

Design tip

Always consider colour in your design. Here the white of the *Magnolia* dominates the subtle hues of pink and purple but the darker colours are repeated in the colour of the inner vase and the shade of burgundy in the tulips.

Most magnolias burst into flower before the leaves unfurl. It is a wonderful sight in the garden but you can take just three flowers and create a design for the home.

Method

1 Entwine the birch stems in the hand and place to fit the larger of the two containers.

2 Put the small decorative glass container in the centre of the larger container. Add water to both.

3 Float the *Magnolia* flowers in the outer container and place two tulips in the central vase.

Glorious *Ranunculus*

You will need

- **low bowl**
- **piece of small gauge chicken wire to fit over the rim of the container**
- **20-30 *Ranunculus***
- **6-10 round, plain green leaves such as *Heuchera*, common ivy (*Hedera*) or *Tellima***

Design tip

Ranunculus leaves deteriorate relatively quickly, faster than the flowers. Removing the leaves and teaming the flowers with a longer lived leaf results in a design easier to maintain. Use plain, rather than variegated leaves, so as to highlight the multitude of tints and tones in the flower heads.

The soft muted colours of the turban flower with their multi-petalled form make a luxurious mass of delicate blooms.

Method

1 Make a template of the bowl's opening with the chicken wire and cut so that it is slightly larger. Bend the excess over the rim and it will stay in place easily (Techniques page 96).

2 Half fill the bowl with water.

3 Remove the leaves from the *Ranunculus*. Cut them and thread them through the grid so that the stem ends reach the water easily.

4 Tuck in a few leaves to break up the mass and to highlight the flowers.

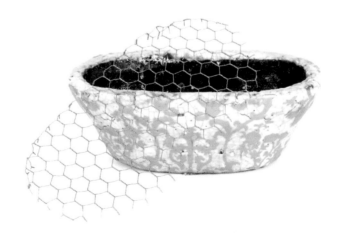

Narcissi topiary

You will need

- **flat dish or plate**
- **pinholder**
- **5-7 bunches of narcissi**
- **rubber band**
- **raffia or string**
- **a few pebbles**

Design tip

If you do not have a pinholder then do not worry. If you use sufficient stems and cut them in a straight line the bunch will probably stand up unaided.

This is one of the simplest ways to display beautiful fragrant *Narcissus*.

Method

1 Arrange the narcissi in your hand so that their stems are straight and their heads form a gentle dome. Roll a rubber band half way up the stems to secure. Tie a length of raffia over the rubber band.

2 Place the pinholder in the centre of the dish. Press the central stems of your topiary firmly onto the pins so that the outer stems obscure the pinholder.

3 Arrange the pebbles on the dish and add a little water.

Flowers in a bowl

You will need

- **broad rimmed bowl about 20 cm (8 in) in diameter**
- **about 30 leaves from the spotted laurel (*Aucuba japonica*)**
- **2 bunches grape hyacinth (*Muscari*)**
- **5-9 double cream tulips**

Design tip

Aucuba japonica **is one of the easiest shrubs to grow. It is tolerant of aspect, drought, water-logging and wind. It also absorbs pollution so it is a must for any front garden.**

The proportions in this design are reversed with the smooth textured, wide rimmed bowl taking dominance over the mix of spring flowers contained within.

Method

1 Cut off the individual leaves of the spotted laurel from the main stem. Mass them together at the back of the bowl.

2 Arrange the grape hyacinths to one side so that the stems lean over the broad rim of the bowl.

3 Fill in the space between the laurel and the grape hyacinth with the double tulips.

All in a twist

The undulating, sinuous curve of the tulips are shown to advantage in this contemporary design.

You will need

· **square cube container**
· **floral foam**
· **twining stems or branches such as those of the Chinese gooseberry or kiwi fruit (*Actinidia*). You could also use dragon's claw willow or contorted hazel.**
· **about 20 tulips**
· **decorative wire**
· **7 *Aspidistra* leaves or other smooth textured foliage**

Design tip

Tulips continue to grow once cut. This will not detract from this design which should last for at least a week. When the tulips are dead remove them but keep the structure in place and replace your tulips for a continuous display.

Method

1 Position wet floral foam in the container so that it is level with the top of the cube.

2 Insert the ends of the *Actinidia* stems in the foam to create a balanced mass.

3 Add the tulips to the design. Some may have their ends in foam, others may be held in place on the branches with decorative wire attached to the stems.

4 Manipulate the *Aspidistra* leaves (Techniques page 97) and position close to the foam to cover. Alternatively insert short stems of other smooth textured foliage.

54

Natural grid

You will need

- **square container**
- **straight stems of *Cornus*, willow or snakegrass (*Equisetum hyemale*)**
- **twine, raffia or paper-covered wire**
- **daffodils**

Design tip

Make sure the holes in the grid are the right size to support the heads of the daffodils or they may fall through the gaps.

This grid structure is simple to make and will last for many months.

Method

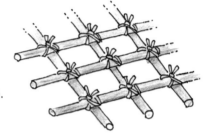

1 Create the grid by binding the sticks together with the twine, raffia or paper-covered wire at right angles to make a square. Add more sticks across the centre. Make sure that the grid fits neatly on top of your chosen container.

2 Add water and cut the daffodils so that their stems are the same length or shorter than the depth of the container. Position the daffodils in the spaces of the grid.

Bed of carnations

This design would make an interesting alternative to a bunch of roses on Valentine's Day and is bold enough to be a gift any man would be proud to receive.

You will need

- square piece of foam
- black plastic bag
- tape or mossing pins
- large rubber band
- length of raffia
- lichen twigs
- red spray carnations (*Dianthus*)
- 1 red rose such as *Rosa* 'Passion', *Rosa* 'Grand Prix', or *Rosa* 'Torero'

Design tip

Spray carnations can be awkward to arrange effectively but if you cut the stems short and make the most of their colour, form and texture, the result is delightful.

Method

1 Cut a square of plastic bag to cover the base and sides of your foam and secure it with tape or mossing pins. This will prevent water contact with any surface.

2 Place the rubber band over the foam so that it is tight.

3 Cut the lichen twigs so that they are slightly taller than the foam and insert them under the rubber band.

4 When you have completed the square, cover the rubber band with the raffia and tie securely.

5 Place your rose into the foam off-centre. Cut the spray carnation heads short and use them to cover the rest of the foam.

Pencil pot

You will need

- **straight-sided tumbler, approximately 15 cm (6 in) tall**
- **coloured drawing pencils**
- **strong rubber band**
- **coloured raffia**
- **brightly coloured tulips**

Design tip

This container would look even brighter if you used felt tip pens, but make sure you ask your children's permission to use them first!

This brightly coloured design is easy enough for a child to make and would look lovely in a playroom.

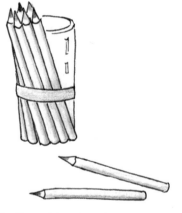

Method

1 Place the rubber band around the middle of the container.

2 Start adding the pencils underneath the rubber band, with their points facing upwards. You will find that they naturally slant diagonally. If you would prefer the pencils to stand up straight then simply add more.

3 Tie the raffia around the container to hide the rubber band.

4 Add your tulips. Choose flowers that pick up the strong primary colours of the pencils.

You will need

- · neutral coloured water tight container
- · 10-20 stems of narcissi
- · 20-25 stems of *Iris*
- · 10-12 stems of pussy willow (*Salix*)

Design tip

Narcissi will poison other flowers with their sap if left to their own devices. To prevent this, leave them on their own in water for 24 hours, then wipe the ends with kitchen towel before mixing with other flowers.

Spring fling

This design provides a burst of colour and is the ideal way to display *Iris*. The neutral colour of the *Salix* matches that of the container, thus tying the design together.

Method

1 Cut the *Iris* so that they sit one and a half times the height of the vase. Cut the narcissi a little shorter and insert them below the *Iris*.

2 Add the *Salix* to the design to add height.

Hatching flowers

The technique of blowing eggs takes a little time to master but once achieved you have the perfect containers for this time of year.

Method

1 Using a drawing pin, make a tiny hole in each end of the egg. Make the hole at the thinner end of the egg slightly larger. Blow hard through the smaller hole and the egg will come out of the larger hole.

2 Cut some raffia into short lengths and place in the bottom of the cubes.

3 Place a knob of fix to the hole at the base of the egg to make it watertight. Fill the eggs with water and place the *Ranunculus* through the holes in the top of the eggs.

You will need

· **3 small glass cube containers**
· **raffia**
· **3 blown eggs**
· **florists' fix**
· **3 *Ranunculus***

Design tip

There are many flowers that would suit this design, but be sure to choose a flower with a slim stem so that it is easy to insert into the hole in the egg.

Heart of roses

You will need

- heart shaped box – this one is 7.5 cm (3 in) long and 7.5 cm (3 in) at the widest point
- plastic bin liner
- small piece of foam
- 3 multi-petalled red roses. I have used *Rosa* 'Grand Prix'.
- stems of green 'santini' (small spray *Chrysanthemum*)

Design tip

If your box is bigger and you have a gap between the roses and the 'santini', increase the number of roses used or create a double row with the 'santini'. If you have a larger container you could alternatively use heads from the larger spray *Chrysanthemum* rather than the 'santini' *Chrysanthemum*.

A simple token for Valentine's Day.

Method

1 Line the box with bin liner cut to fit the base and sides.

2 Soak and fit a piece of foam inside the container so that it rises to just below the rim.

3 Cut the three roses short and place centrally, following the heart shape of the box.

4 Cut the individual heads off the 'santini' and place each one tight to the rim of the box to create a surround.

Egg-cellence

Create this nest for Easter which will last for months – remove the eggs after the holiday and you have a lovely spring wreath.

You will need

- a foam ring of a size to fit your table
- 3-6 stems of pussy willow (*Salix discolor*)
- florists' wire
- conifer or another long lasting evergreen
- 12-16 painted eggs
- green and yellow feathers (optional)

Design tips

If fresh pussy willow is used to create designs and kept out of water, it will keep its furry tips indefinitely. If kept in water the tips will develop and eventually drop.

If the willow is stiff, then immerse it under water for an hour and it will become more flexible.

Method

1 Wet the foam ring by placing it at an angle in water with the foam uppermost.

2 Create a ring of pussy willow that will fit neatly around the foam ring. Fresh willow is flexible and can be easily wired in place with florists' wire to make a secure ring.

3 Cover the foam with short sprigs of conifer so it lies reasonably flat and moves in the same circular direction.

4 Fill the centre with painted or chocolate eggs. Tuck in a few feathers for seasonal effect.

5 If you wish to move the arrangement place a tin lid or plate under the foam ring so that the eggs are contained.

Daffodil spiral

You will need

- **low dish**
- **around 20 daffodils (*Narcissus*)**
- **large pinholder, ideally 7.5 cm (3 in)**
- **aggregates such as slate chips**

Design tip

For this design you need daffodils in their prime. Double daffodils are easier to use because they will last so much longer and their heads are more consistently at the same angle.

The swirl of daffodils in this design gives focus to every flower and stem.

Method

1 Lay the daffodils on a work surface. The stem end of the longest should be positioned so that it reaches the edge of the table but does not protude.

2 The other daffodils should be positioned so that every head is just a little shorter than the one before. Cut the stems level with the edge of the table.

3 Place the longest stem in the centre of the pinholder. Place the second stem so the head rests close to the first but at a slightly lower level. Repeat with the other daffodils, turning the arrangement as you go. You will achieve a spiral of daffodils. Stop about 5 cm (2 in) from the base so that there is a small amount of the final stems showing.

4 Disguise the pinholder using the aggregates and add water.

Tube of tulips

You will need

- **empty crisp tube**
- **spray glue or spray mount**
- **fabric to cover the container**
- **6-8 tulips**

Design tip

The tube I have used is watertight. If using any other type then be sure to check that it does not leak.

Creating your own vase out of a crisp tube and an off-cut of fabric is a simple and rewarding exercise. It costs next to nothing and is an easy way to coordinate the vase to your interior.

Method

1 Make sure the crisp tube is clean and dry.

2 Place the tube on its side on the fabric and measure how much you will need. Leave a little excess at either end – enough to wrap the container with 2.5 cm (1 in) extra. Cut the material.

3 Cover the tube liberally with spray mount, making sure you are in a well ventilated area. Leave it to dry a little until the glue is tacky to the touch.

4 Lay the tube on the fabric and wrap it tightly. Smooth down the material so that there are no lumps or wrinkles.

5 Cut off the excess material and neatly fold in the ends.

6 Add water to the tube and arrange your tulips within.

Chic and simple

You will need

- **round plate with sides sufficiently deep to hold the coil**
- **roll of trellised plant material such as *Clematis*. If this is hard to find, then coloured mesh by OASIS® or chicken wire cut into a long strip will also work well.**
- **1 plastic or glass orchid tube**
- **1 head of *Cymbidium* orchid**

Design tip

Any strong flower in terms of form and colour will work in this design. Examples are a marigold, *Dahlia*, rose or mini *Gerbera*. Choose your colour to co-ordinate with the interior of your room.

Minimalist and simple, this design uses a single flower to give stunning impact.

Method

1 Place the coil on the plate. Allow the coil to expand to fill the space.

2 Fill the orchid tube with water and insert the single stem so that the stem barely protrudes above the rim.

3 Position the orchid between the coils. These will provide support. To give good balance place the flower at the opposite side to the open end of the coil as this creates strong visual pull.

Cherry blossom

You will need

- tall cylindrical glass vase
- stems of straight *Prunus*
- 1 tulip in a colour to co-ordinate

Design tip

Ensure that the water is sufficiently low that none of the cherry blossom flowers are under water. If they are, they will rapidly deteriorate and cause bacteria to multiply more quickly.

Cherry blossom (*Prunus*) sold as a cut flower has a straight form that is ideal for massing within a straight-sided container.

Method

1 Place a small amount of water in the vase.

2 Cut the long stems of cherry blossom into shorter lengths that are the same height as the container. Position these around the inner circumference of the vase.

3 Place the single stem of tulip in the centre of the cherry blossom.

Spring soup

This is the perfect way to use all those odds and ends from the garden.

Method
Cut the flowers as short as possible and float in water.

Design tip

Use flowers that are happy floating in water. This includes most spring flowers. Use at least one flower with a strong form and/or colour – here the narcissi – to give focal dominance.

75

Currant display

You will need

- **square glass tank**
- **piece of foam**
- **dried flat seed pods**
- **5 tulips**

Design tips

Many say that the smell of *Ribes* is unpleasant. If you do not like the fragrance, place the cut stems outdoors for 24 hours by which time the smell will have diminished.

Cinnamon sticks or dogwood (*Cornus*) stems could be used instead of the seed pods.

Flowering currant (*Ribes sanguineum*) has been a mainstay of the British garden for many years. Although deciduous it is one of the first shrubs to burst into leaf, shortly followed by pendulous, fragrant pink flowers.

Method

1 Cut and soak a piece of foam to fit low inside the tank so that it allows the insertion of the pods all the way around. The foam does not need to be tall as its purpose is primarily to keep the pods in position and not fall into the centre.

2 Place the pods between the foam and the glass.

3 Cut the stems of *Ribes* and create a mass about the height of the container above the rim.

4 Add the tulips.

Queen Anne's lace

You will need

- stems of Queen Anne's lace (*Anthriscus sylvestris*)
- tall slim container
- low bowl

Design tip

You could create a similar sort of design with *Gypsophila* or wild fennel (*Foeniculum vulgare*) during the summer or Michaelmas daisies in the autumn.

This wonderful weed can be gathered from the river banks and hedgerows to create glorious large arrangements at no cost. The name arose in the days when Queen Anne used to travel the country in May, when the flower is abundant in the hedgerows. People believed that the roads had been decorated specially for her.

Method

1 Place the tall container in the centre of the low bowl. Half fill both with water.

2 Remove the low side shoots from the stems.

3 Position the side shoots around the low bowl.

4 Arrange the main stems in the tall container ensuring that none of the flowers are below the water line.

Egg plant

Budding branches and a few plastic eggs are all you need to create a stunning Easter arrangement.

You will need

- ceramic container
- floral foam
- slender branches coming into new life
- sisal
- plastic Easter eggs
- florists' wire

Design tip

Plastic eggs can create a stunning garden feature if hung from a small tree in the garden. Painted eggs rather than plastic eggs can also be used in the home.

Method

1 Soak the foam and pack into the container so that it rises gently above the rim.

2 Impale the twigs in the foam.

3 Loosely cover the foam with the sisal.

4 Pass a wire through the loop at the end of each egg and twist to form a short stem.

5 Place the wired eggs around the sides of the foam to create a circle. They should rest on the small gap between the foam and the container so that they do not protrude too far over the rim.

6 Hang the remaining eggs from the branches.

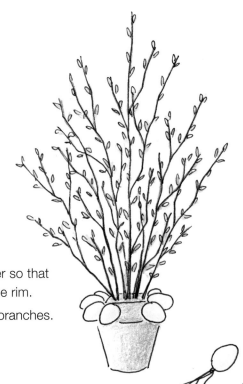

Candy coloured tulips

Strong bright colours are a lively fun approach to flower arranging.

You will need

· **rectangular glass tank**
· **mass of eggs to fill the container. Mine were plastic and had the annoying habit of floating so I needed quite a few to give ballast!**
· **tulips**
· **florists' tape or garden twine**

Design tip

If you use painted eggs check that they are not going to smudge under water. You may wish to use a tumbler or jam jar centrally, filled with water for the tulips, and to mass the eggs around.

Method

1 Pour water into the container and add the eggs.

2 Clean the stems of the tulips and remove any excess leaves.

3 Group the tulips in the hand and trim the ends so that the stems are neat. Bind with tape or tie with twine.

4 Push the stems through the eggs and into the water.

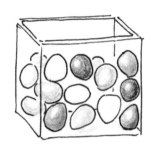

Winter into spring

You will need

- **low glass bowl**
- **tall glass vase**
- **about 20 tulips – the ones used are called *Tulipa* 'Yokohama'**
- **5 blue hyacinths**
- **lichen covered twigs (optional)**
- **10 *Ranunculus***

Design tips

Spring flowers love close contact with water and cutting the stems of the *Ranunculus* so short will actually lengthen their life.

You could float anemones or hyacinth florets instead of the *Ranunculus*.

Dried lichen twigs are combined with spring flowers to take winter into spring.

Method

1 Place the tall vase in the centre of the low bowl and add water to both.

2 Arrange the tulips in the hand so that the stems spiral in the same direction. This can be easily achieved by crossing each stem over the one placed before.

3 The hyacinth stems will be shorter than the tulips so thread these through once the bunch of tulips is in place.

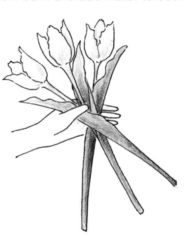

4 Cut the ends of the flowers and place in the vase.

5 Add the lichen twigs through the design.

6 Cut the heads of the *Ranunculus* and let them float on the water in the low bowl.

Stark and simple

You will need

- roll of bamboo matting
- rubber band
- *Aspidistra* leaf
- length of raffia
- 6-9 glass test tubes
- 9-12 stems *Ranunculus*

Design tips

Fragrant *Narcissus* also look great in this design.

Glass tubes are often larger than the plastic ones and more decorative (even if you are only seeing a small amount). If you cannot acquire glass tubes buy the plastic ones which many florists are happy to give away if you are a regular customer.

This innovative arrangement converts a length of bamboo matting and turns it into a contemporary container. The clean lines of the *Ranunculus* stems repeat the upward movement of the container and the bold form of the red flowers give strength and impact.

Method

1 Roll the bamboo matting and secure in place with a wide rubber band.

2 Wrap an *Aspidistra* leaf around the rubber band and secure with raffia.

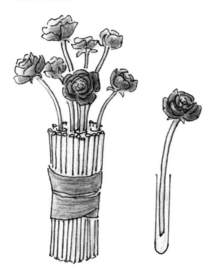

3 Fill the tubes with water and push into the rolled matting. The rims should be level with the top of the matting which is flexible and will grip the tubes easily and securely.

4 Remove the foliage from the *Ranunculus* and place in the tubes.

Floral lace

A tracery of floral lace can be created with just a few strands of long lasting *Genista*.

You will need

- **round glass bowl**
- **small piece of foam**
- **half stem ming fern (*Asparagus umbellatus*) or 1 stem of small leaved foliage such as box (*Buxus*)**
- **1 stem of broom (*Genista*)**
- **1 rose**

Design tip

Here the *Rosa* 'Cool Water' links with the colour of the broom to give a harmonious colour-link. If you use yellow broom try *Rosa* 'Sonrisa' or *Rosa* 'Sphinx'. If white, *Rosa* 'Avalanche' or *Rosa* 'Bianca'. All these roses named are beautiful, reliable and long lasting.

Method

1 Place a small piece of soaked foam at the bottom of the glass bowl.

2 Cover the foam with small snippets of ming fern or other foliage.

3 Cut strands of broom off the main stem. Insert one end of each strand in the foam and allow to 'climb' up the sides of the bowl.

4 Cut the rose short and place centrally. The stem should be hidden.

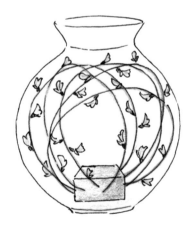

Lily-of-the-valley

You will need

- **small cut glass tumbler or vase**
- **lily-of-the-valley (Convallaria majalis) – as many stems as you can afford or can take easily from the garden**
- **small delicate round leaves such as those of the Cyclamen or Heuchera**

Design tip

When choosing a vase for these ephemeral flowers, pottery was too heavy, plain glass too ordinary, aluminum too contrived, but the cut glass was just right.

Intensely fragrant, the delicate bells of this elegant flower are shown to advantage in cut glass with just a few leaves at the rim to make them go further.

Method

1 Cut the stems of the lily-of-the-valley and place in your container. Only cut off the minimum length, as the longer the stems the more graceful the flowers.

2 Place the leaves around the rim of the container. Ensure that the stem ends are in water.

Techniques

General guidelines for arranging

Form

As a general guide most flowers can be classified as being round (such as a *Gerbera*, peony, sunflower, *Dahlia*), spray (such as *Limonium*, *Gypsophila*, *Hypericum*, spray carnation) or linear (*Delphinium*, gladioli, lavender). Round flowers are the key players. They are the most dominant form in design and should be included in all work using mixed flowers (see pages 9, 45). Spray flowers are the supporting actors and give softness and interest to the design (see pages 31, 35). Linear flowers are important in minimalist and large scale work and parallel designs (see page 42).

Colour

Colour is personal and subjective. However plain green is nature's harmonizer and in sufficient quantities makes any combination of mixed flowers look good. Lime green gives zing and blue adds depth and interest to any design. The colour yellow advances and can be seen most easily at a distance and in poor light. Blues and purples are recessive and should not be used in designs in a large setting, especially if the light is poor.

Texture

Texture is how you imagine something will appear to the touch, e.g. rough, prickly, feathery. Always include one texture that is smooth (such as *Aspidistra*, *Fatsia*, ivy, roses or poppy seedheads) into your designs of mixed plant material.

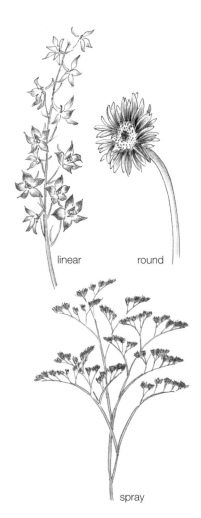

linear   round

spray

Balance

The majority of work shown enjoys symmetrical balance, i.e. if an imaginary line is drawn down the centre the visual weight each side will appear equal. It is vital that your work does not fall over and does not appear to be falling over so ensure it is balanced top to bottom, side to side and front to back.

Proportion

The good use of proportion applies most obviously to vase work where the volume of plant material to the volume of container should be 1.5 : 1 or 1 : 1.5 if the container is of special interest and the most important part of the design. Alternatively, the ratio of the *height* of the plant material to that of container should be 1.5 : 1 if only a few vertical flowers are used. In the design on page 33 the height of the flowers to the width of the container is 1.5 : 1.

Floral foam

Using floral foam

Floral foam is a water absorbing material which supports stems at virtually any angle. It is readily available at DIY stores, florists and larger supermarkets. OASIS® is a well-known brand name. Floral foam is most commonly available in a brick-sized block but is also available in cones, cylinders, rings, spheres and many other shapes. There is also a coloured foam called OASIS® Rainbow® Foam. This takes much longer to soak and does not contain cut flower food.

Preparing foam

Cut the piece of foam you require and place it horizontally on water that is deeper than the piece of foam you wish to soak. Allow the foam to sink under its own weight until the top if level with the water and the colour has changed from light to dark green. Keep topped up with water.

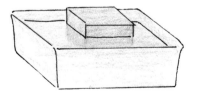

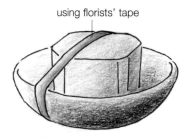

using florists' tape

Securing foam in container

To secure foam in a container you can either:

- Place florists' fix on the base of a four pronged disc called a 'frog'.
- Place this on the clean, dry surface of your container and impale your soaked foam on the frog.

or

- Use florists' tape across the top of your foam and down the two sides of the container.

Storing foam

Store foam that has been soaked in a tied plastic bag. In this way the foam will remain wet and keep for ages. If soaked foam is left in the open air it will dry out and will not take up further supplies of water.

Alternative stem supports

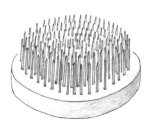

Pinholders

Pinholders, or kenzans as they are sometimes known, are stem supports (otherwise known as a mechanic). They are ideal for:

- spring flowers with soft stems that have a need for copious amounts of water such as anemones, *Ranunculus* and daffodils
- woody stems that are often too heavy to stay happily in place in floral foam, such as lilac (*Syringa*) and guelder rose (*Viburnum opulus* 'Roseum')

Pinholders may be purchased in a wide variety of sizes from the minute 1.5 cm (½ in) to the large 15 cm (6 in). The most easily found is 6.5 cm (2½ in). A pinholder consists of a multitude of short metal pins in a heavy base which is usually, but not always, round.

The Japanese rarely use a fixative on the base of a kenzan but for the novice it makes life easier if you place a coil of florists' fix on the base of the pinholder and position it firmly on a clean dry base. You could alternatively cut a piece of rubber, or the packing that is placed under packaged meats from the supermarket, to fit under the pinholder.

Spring flowers can be simply cut and impaled on the pinholder. Woody stems need to be cut at an angle and, if you wish, make a short slit up from the base. The angled cut of the stem should face away from the direction in which the branch is to lean.

If your stems are thin – such as those of the *Freesia* – tie them together with wool before placing on the pin holder or wedge with a woody stem.

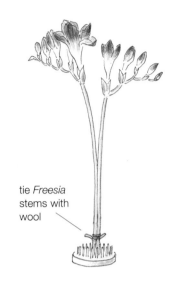

tie *Freesia* stems with wool

Adhesive tape

For glass containers transparent adhesive tape can be used to create a grid over the opening to give support. You can use tape available from stationers; it will work well as long as it is suitably narrow. There is also a specialist clear tape available that is waterproof and may be worth buying if you often work with glass.

Tubes

Glass test tubes such as the ones used on pages 86–87 are a useful way to use spring flowers in more structural and unusual designs and still give them the water that they love. You can also obtain plastic tubes with lids through which a stem can be inserted – these are often used for orchids. These are less attractive but there are various methods of disguising them (such as wrapping them with small leaves or moss). They are available in a variety of sizes. They also have the advantage that they can be secured at any angle and will not spill their contents. Some glass tubes are now manufactured with holes at the rim for hanging.

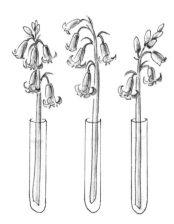

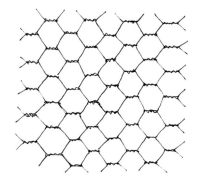

Chicken wire (wire netting)

Chicken wire, sometimes known as wire netting, used inside a container is the ideal method of securing soft stems and flowers which need a lot of water such as spring flowers.

A good mesh size for this purpose is the 5 cm (2 in). The amount you use depends to some extent on the size of the container and the thickness of the stems you wish to insert. A rough guideline would be to cut a piece a little wider than the width of the opening and three times the depth. Cut off the selvedge as this is stiff. Crumple the netting so that it forms approximately the same shape as the container.

Fill the container with water and thread your stems through the chicken wire. If the mesh of your wire is small the holes will disappear to nothing once you have several layers.

If you need extra support, particularly if you are using thick stemmed heavy branches, place a pinholder in the bottom of your container. Allow your first placement through the chicken wire to be well impaled on the pinholder and this will secure the netting firmly.

You can also use a single layer over the opening of the container. To do this cut a piece of 1 cm (½ in) or 2.5 cm (1 in) chicken wire, approximately 1 cm larger than the area you wish to cover. Place this over the opening and fold the surplus down over the edges. This method is useful for stems that need only a little support.

Other techniques

Manipulating leaves

There are many ways to manipulate leaves but the method we have used on page 55 uses an *Aspidistra* leaf which is manipulated in the following way. Fold the tip of the *Aspidistra* down to the point where the leaf meets the stalk. Angle it to one side. Take the stem and bring it backwards and over so that it can be pushed through the two layers of the folded leaf. To do this the stems needs to be reasonably long.

Blowing eggs

Use a pin to make a hole in both ends of the egg, one slightly larger than the other. Blow hard into the smaller hole so the egg comes out into a bowl or other container. Rinse the egg in cold water and place on a piece of tissue to dry.

Cleaning glass vases

With regular use glass vases can become clouded and grimy. A useful tool for cleaning them is a denture cleaning tablet which will remove all dirt and leave the vase sparkling. Smaller vases will go in the dishwasher if the glass is of uniform thickness but will break if the glass is of different densities. You can also buy special vase cleaning tablets.

Submersion

There are some flowers, fruit and vegetables that will last underwater and others that will decompose rapidly. Flowers suited to submersion include orchids, roses and hydrangeas. Hard or thick skinned fruits which would be suitable include kumquats, crab apples and quince.

Buying spring flowers

- Buy tulips that show some colour. If no colour is showing they will rarely open.

- Powdery dark pollen on anemones show that they are mature and therefore nearing the end of their life. Buy anemones before the heads are fully open and flat.

- *Camellia* foliage is fantastic – the waxy leaves shine and are incredibly long lasting. Take care not to purchase if the leaves seem to be covered in black dirt. This is actually a sooty mould that is difficult to remove.

- Purchase the first quality terminal branches of broom (*Genista*) rather than the second quality woody stems.

- The fluffy fragrant heads of mimosa (*Acacia*) usually have cellophane protection. This is to stop the flowers drying out which they do rapidly in a dry or draughty environment.

- Purchase *Freesia* when at least one bud is showing colour. This is particularly appropriate in the colder months of the year.

- Purchase lily-of-the-valley (*Convallaria majalis*) only when the top bell is showing good colour, otherwise it may not open.

- Grape hyacinths (*Muscari*) have a short life so buy when only a few of the lower flowers are open.

- Buy peonies (*Paeonia*) in bud when the colour of the petals is showing.

- Once cut the flowering head of the tulip grows more rapidly than the foliage. Purchase tulips where the flower is at a level with the leaves and not where the flower soars centimetres above.

Caring for your flowers

- Tulips, *Ranunculus* and anemones are heavy drinkers so always ensure they have a supply of water.

- Hellebores will last many weeks but only when the seeds have formed in the centre of the flower and the stamens have disappeared.

- Keep broom (*Genista*) away from ripening fruits and vegetables as it is particularly susceptible to the ethylene gas that they generate.

- Remove the dead flowers on the raceme of *Freesia* as this will encourage flowers further up the stem to open.

- Try and keep the bulbous white ends of the hyacinth on the stem as they contain food which continues to nourish the flower.

- The flowers of lily-of-the-valley will wilt quickly if left in a warm atmosphere.

- If you wish to keep your peonies from opening, store them in a box out of water, where they can be kept for up to five days without harm. They will open once they are placed in water.

- Anemones love their faces in water. If they look to be wilting cut their stems short and float them in water.

- The guelder rose (*Viburnum opulus* 'Roseum') and lilac (*Syringa*) produce masses of foliage along with the flowering head. In order for water to travel to the flower you need to remove 90 percent of the foliage before cutting the stem at a sharp angle and placing in water – ideally adding a special cut shrub food.

- Tulips curve towards the light so arrange them in a position which gets even light.

Flower index

A selection of flowers available during the Spring months.

Blue and Purple

Astrantia
(great masterwort)
also available in
pink, white,
burgundy

Centaurea montana
(cornflower)
also available in
white

Iris
also available in
yellow, purple, white

Muscari
(grape hyacinth)
also available in pink,
white

Red and Pink

Anemone
also available in
blue, purple, white

Cornus (dogwood)
also available in
green, orange, yellow
(F)

Dianthus (carnation)
also available in
many colours

Freesia (freesia)
also available in
many colours

Key: (F) = foliage

Myosotis
(forget-me-not)

Ranunculus
(turban flower)
also available in
orange, yellow, pink,
white, red

Syringa (lilac)
also available in
pink, white

Trachelium
also available in
green, white

Veronica
also available in
pink, white

Helleborus
(hellebore)
also available in
red,white,green

Hyacinthus (hyacinth)
also available in
pink, orange, white,
yellow, blue, purple

Ixia (African corn lily)

Rosa 'Grand Prix'

Tulipa (tulip)
also available in
many colours

Orange and Yellow

Acacia (mimosa)

Alstroemeria
(Peruvian lily)
also available in
many colours

Genista (broom)
also available in pink,
white

Narcissus
also available in
white

White and Cream

Anthurium
(flamingo flower)
also available in red,
brown, pink, yellow,
green, bi-coloured

Chamelaucium
(wax flower)
also available in pink

Convallaria majalis
(lily of the valley)
also available in
pink

Eustoma (lisianthus)
also available in
pink, blue, purple

Green

Cornus (dogwood)
(F)

Cymbidium orchid
also available in
many colours

Euphorbia
(sun spurge)

Helleborus foetidus
(hellebore)

Narcissus (daffodil)
also available in
white, pink

Ranunculus
(turban flower)
also available in
white, pink, red,
purple

Rosa 'Radio!'

Rosa 'Toscanini'

Zantedeschia
(calla lily)
also available in
many colours

Paeonia (peony)
also available in
pink, red, bi-colours

Polygonatum
(Solomon's seal)

Prunus
(cherry blossom)
also available in pink

Salix (pussy willow)
(F)

Tulipa (frilly tulip)
also available in
many colours

Skimmia
also available in
red (F)

Sorbus aria
(whitebeam) (F)

Tulipa (parrot tulip)

Tulipa
tulip seed pod

Viburnum opulus
'Roseum'
(snowball tree)

Glossary

Aggregates
Coloured gravel or small stones used to add texture as well as to hide mechanics at little expense.

Aluminum wire
A very flexible wire available in a wide variety of colours and thicknesses. It is soft enough to cut with scissors.

Bullion or Boullion wire
A fine decorative wire with a curl or bend to it that gives a fine shimmer to designs.

Decorative wire
Available in many different colours and thickness, this wire is used to add colour and create other decorative effects. You can buy this from craft shops and garden centres.

Florists' fix
An adhesive putty that is purchased on a roll. It must be used on a clean dry surface so that it will stick firmly.

Florists' tape
A strong tape that can be purchased in various widths. It is strong and waterproof.

Frog
A green plastic disc with four prongs that comes in both large and small sizes. Ideal used in conjunction with fix to secure foam.

Glass vases
Available in every shape and size imaginable and do not have to be expensive. The ideal size to own is 20 cm (8 in) tall. Other useful vases are a cube, two tanks – one that sits inside the other with space between, a fishbowl and a tall thin vase.

Mossing pins
Also known as German pins, these are used for securing plant material to foam. Create your own by taking a stub wire and bending it in two.

Orchid tubes

Orchids are often supplied to florists in short plastic tubes with a rubber top with a hole for the stem. Your florist may let you have these as they are often thrown away. They are also available from craft shops.

Raffia

This may be purchased in a natural tone or in a wide range of dyed colours. Raffia can be looped, made into bows or tied round containers and bunches to give a natural look.

Shells

Available in a variety of sizes, shapes and colours. You can purchase them in bags from a craft shop.

Sisal

Sisal is a natural material derived from *Agave sisalana* leaves. It is available in a wide range of colours and is very useful filler.

Spray mount

Spray mount or spray glue allows you to reposition items as often as you wish. Sprayed lightly it will not seep through and damage fabric.

Stem tape

This is used to disguise wires that have been added to extend or give support to fresh plant material. It also slows down the evaporation of water from the stem.

Stub wires

Lengths of wire (as opposed to wire on a reel) used in floristry for extending, supporting or replacing stems. Wires are measured by gauge – the higher the gauge the thicker and less flexible the wire. The wire used must be the lightest possible needed to support the head of the flower you are wiring.

Table Decos

A narrow plastic tray with foam pre-attached. Available in three different lengths – mini, medi and maxi. They are useful for parallel designs.

NB

Many of the items mentioned in the Glossary can be purchased from Hobbycraft in the UK (www.hobbycraft.co.uk) and from Michaels in the USA (www.michaels.com).

The Judith Blacklock Flower School

The Judith Blacklock Flower School offers intensive, structured courses in all aspects of flower arranging and the business of floristry. In a quiet secluded mews in Knightsbridge, London, Judith and her team of dedicated teachers give professional information and practical learning skills, using the most beautiful flowers and foliage, that are relevant to participants from all over the world.

From basic design through to the most advanced contemporary work there is a course suitable for every level of expertise.

Private, team building and structured group lessons are available on request.

The Judith Blacklock Flower School
4/5 Kinnerton Place South, London SW1X 8EH
Tel. +44 (0)20 7235 6235
school@judithblacklock.com
www.judithblacklock.com

Acknowledgements

Photography

All photographs are by Tobias Smith www.tobiassmith.com
except for
Judith Blacklock: pages 23, 75
Scott Forrester: pages 54, 55
Lyndon Parker: pages 6, 7, 8, 9, 36, 37, 63, 84, 85
Rachel Petty: page 109

© iStockphoto.com/Desirée Walstra: page 1
© iStockphoto.com/Leonid Nyshko: page 2
© iStockphoto.com/Chuck Palmer: page 101
© iStockphoto.com/Gina Goforth: page 106

Line Drawings: Tomoko Nakamoto
Botanical Editor: Dr. Christina Curtis
Assistant Editor: Rachel Petty

Thanks to David Austin Roses for the cut roses on page 8.

A big thank you to those who have helped me with ideas, inspiration and practical help. Rachel Petty, who is a wiz at coming up with inventive titles for the designs, also has great creative skills including blowing eggs. She has put the book and digital photos together and helped enormously. Dawn Jennings is as always an inspiration and my technical manager Chika Yoshida has made the impossible possible.

Tomoko Nakamoto has created more delightful line drawings and Dr. Curtis has checked all the botanical nomenclature with her usual passion and attention to detail. Tobias Smith has taken photographs with care, speed and brilliance for which I thank him. Finally, Amanda Hawkes, the designer of all designers, not only does she create stylish timeless work, but she also works with dignity, patience and kindness, qualities which are much appreciated.